Hello, Body! BONES

by Joyce Markovics

Cherry Lake Press
Ann Arbor, Michigan

Published in the United States of America by Cherry Lake Publishing Group
Ann Arbor, Michigan
www.cherrylakepublishing.com

Reading Adviser: Beth Walker Gambro, MS Ed., Reading Consultant, Yorkville, IL
Content Advisers: Sharon Markovics, MD, and Peter Markovics, MD
Book Designer: Ed Morgan

Photo Credits: freepik.com, 4; freepik.com, 5; freepik.com, 6; The images of Harry Eastlack are used by kind permission of The College of Physicians of Philadelphia, 7; Sabina Music Rich/Unsplash.com, 8; freepik.com, 9; © Bunsinth-Nan-Pua/Shutterstock, 11 top; freepik.com, 11 bottom; © sciencepics/Shutterstock, 12; Wikimedia Commons, 13; © Africa Studio/Shutterstock, 14–15; freepik.com, 16; freepik.com, 17; freepik.com, 18; © Alex Mit/Shutterstock, 19; freepik.com, 20; © Crevis/Shutterstock, 21.

Copyright © 2023 by Cherry Lake Publishing Group

All rights reserved. No part of this book may be reproduced or utilized in any form or by any means without written permission from the publisher.

Cherry Lake Press is an imprint of Cherry Lake Publishing Group.

Library of Congress Cataloging-in-Publication Data

Names: Markovics, Joyce L., author.
Title: Bones / by Joyce Markovics.
Description: Ann Arbor, Michigan : Cherry Lake Publishing, [2023] | Series: Hello, body! | Includes bibliographical references and index. | Audience: Grades 4-6
Identifiers: LCCN 2022003689 (print) | LCCN 2022003690 (ebook) | ISBN 9781668909577 (hardcover) | ISBN 9781668911174 (paperback) | ISBN 9781668912768 (ebook) | ISBN 9781668914359 (pdf)
Subjects: LCSH: Bones–Juvenile literature.
Classification: LCC QM101 .M326 2023 (print) | LCC QM101 (ebook) | DDC 612.7/51–dc23/eng/20220330
LC record available at https://lccn.loc.gov/2022003689
LC ebook record available at https://lccn.loc.gov/2022003690

Printed in the United States of America by
Corporate Graphics

CONTENTS

Two Skeletons 4
Bone Basics 8
Growing Bones 14
Spine Time 18
Brittle Bones 20
  Health Tips 22
  Glossary 23
  Find Out More 24
  Index 24
  About the Author 24

TWO SKELETONS

Harry Eastlack was born in 1933. He had an extra-large big toe. Otherwise, Harry was a healthy baby. At age 4, Harry was hit by a car and broke his leg. Doctors put his leg in a cast. When they took it off, they saw something strange. Harry's leg was painful and swollen.

A short time later, doctors x-rayed Harry's leg. They were stunned when they saw extra bone growing on top of his leg bone. Harry was diagnosed with FOP, a disease that can cause the body to grow two skeletons!

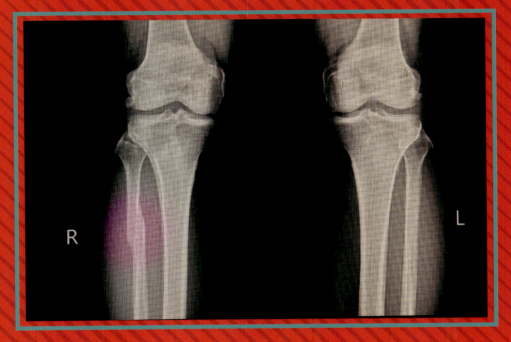

FOP is also called stoneman's disease. People who have FOP are often born with oversized big toes.

FOP stands for fibrodysplasia ossificans progressiva. This very rare disease affects 1 in 2 million people.

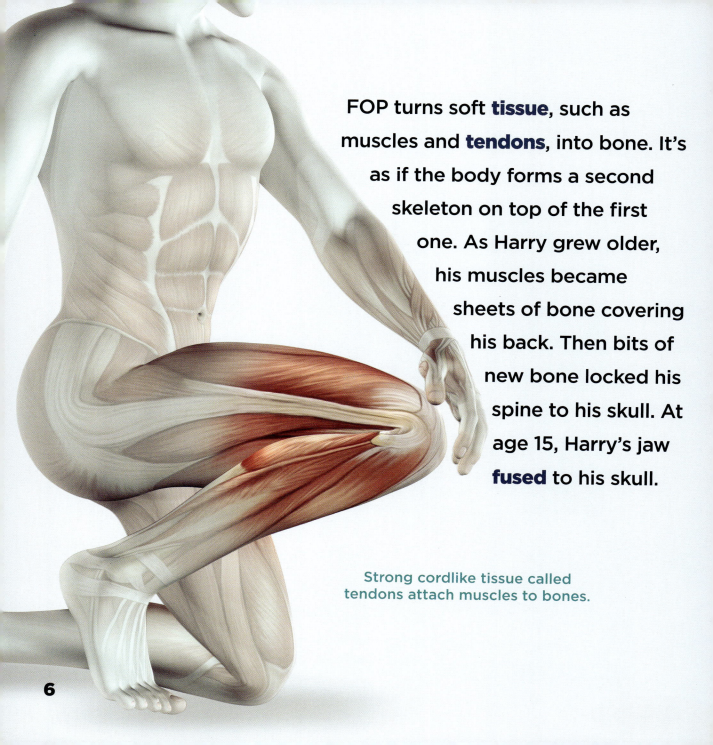

FOP turns soft **tissue**, such as muscles and **tendons**, into bone. It's as if the body forms a second skeleton on top of the first one. As Harry grew older, his muscles became sheets of bone covering his back. Then bits of new bone locked his spine to his skull. At age 15, Harry's jaw **fused** to his skull.

Strong cordlike tissue called tendons attach muscles to bones.

As a result, Harry could no longer open his mouth. He spoke through clenched teeth. Over time, he lost the ability to walk. Despite this, Harry carried on. In 1973, he died from **pneumonia**. Harry gave his body to science. He wanted the world to learn from his special skeleton.

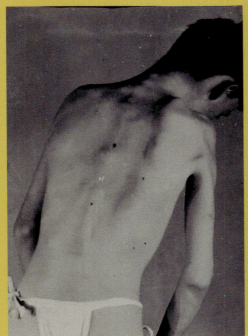 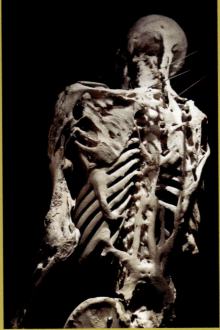

Harry Eastlack's skeleton is on display at The Mütter Museum in Philadelphia. It has helped doctors research FOP for many years.

BONE BASICS

Just like Harry, every person on Earth has a skeleton. Your skeleton is made up of bones—all 206 of them. Bones support your body and give it shape. They also protect your soft internal **organs**. For example, your skull protects your brain. And your ribs form a strong cage around your heart and lungs.

Have you ever seen a skeleton in a museum? The bones probably looked dry and brittle. However, the bones inside your body are the opposite. They're alive—growing and changing all the time, just like you.

> Bones don't weigh a lot. Yet they're strong enough to support our whole bodies.

Lots of foods are rich in calcium, such as greens, milk, beans, and nuts.

What are bones made of? They're mostly made of **collagen**, a type of protein. Bones also include a **mineral** called calcium. Calcium makes your bones hard and strong. It's also needed for muscles to move and for **nerves** to carry messages in your body. Calcium is stored in your bones. When your body needs it, your bones release it into your blood.

We get calcium from eating certain foods. Vitamin D helps our bodies take in calcium from these foods. A lack of vitamin D can lead to bone diseases, such as rickets. Rickets can weaken a child's bones, causing **deformities**.

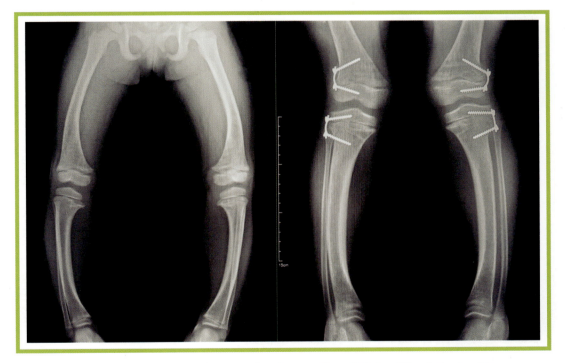

The x-ray on the left shows the legs of a child with rickets. The x-ray on the right shows the same child's legs after treatment.

Even though they seem alike, teeth are not bones. They're made from other materials. However, both are white and store calcium.

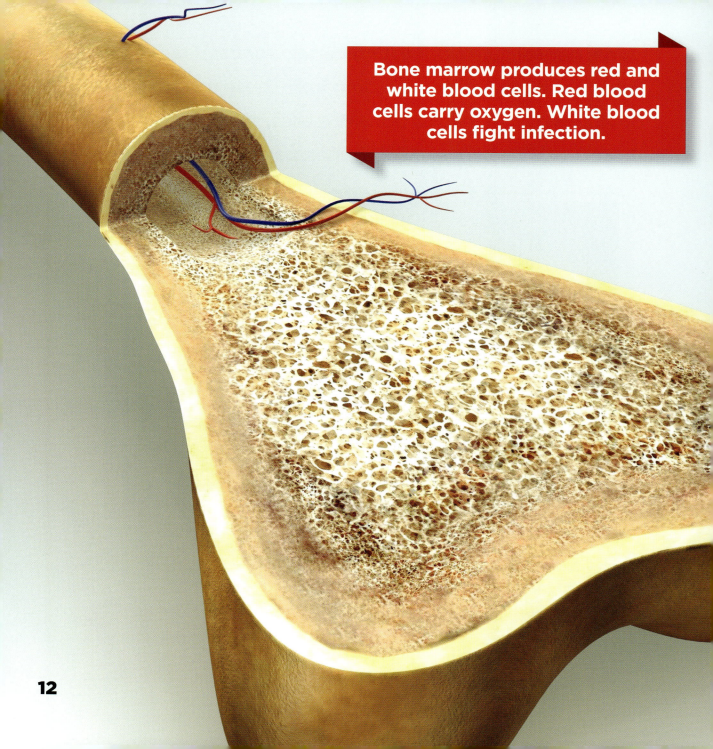

Bone marrow produces red and white blood cells. Red blood cells carry oxygen. White blood cells fight infection.

The bones in your body are not solid. In fact, they have different layers. The outer surface is called the periosteum (pare-ee-OSS-tee-uhm). It's thin, dense, and contains lots of nerves and blood vessels. Below that layer is compact bone. Compact bone is hard and smooth. Cancellous (KAN-suh-lus) bone is the central layer. It's not quite as strong and looks like a sponge. Cancellous bone is made of a network of tiny pieces of bone. Inside this network is soft, jellylike bone marrow. Bone marrow makes the cells that form blood.

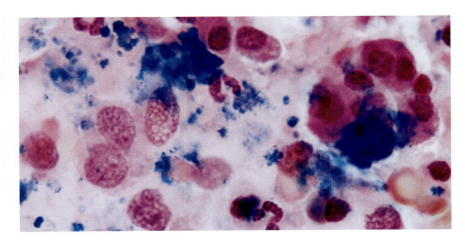

This is a close-up view of bone marrow. Bone marrow makes platelets too. These bits of cells stop us from bleeding too much when we're cut.

GROWING BONES

As a baby, you had tiny fingers and toes. Your bones were small like you. Then as you grew, your bones grew too. At birth, a baby has close to 300 separate bones. However, adults have just 206 bones. As a child gets older, some of these bones grow together. But how?

The bones of babies contain growth plates. These areas consist of cartilage (KAR-tuh-lij). This material is soft, rubbery, and flexible. As babies grow, the cartilage absorbs calcium. Over time, it turns into hard bone.

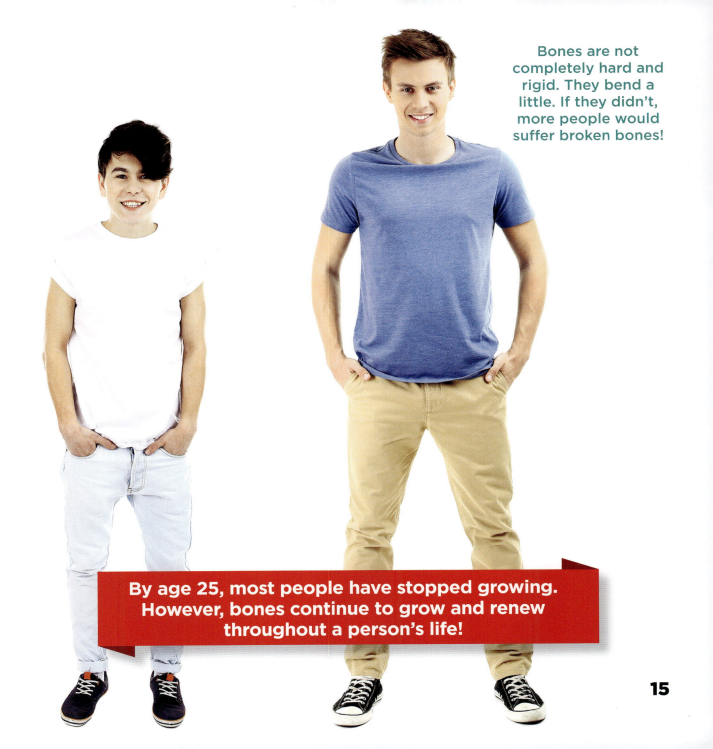

Bones are not completely hard and rigid. They bend a little. If they didn't, more people would suffer broken bones!

By age 25, most people have stopped growing. However, bones continue to grow and renew throughout a person's life!

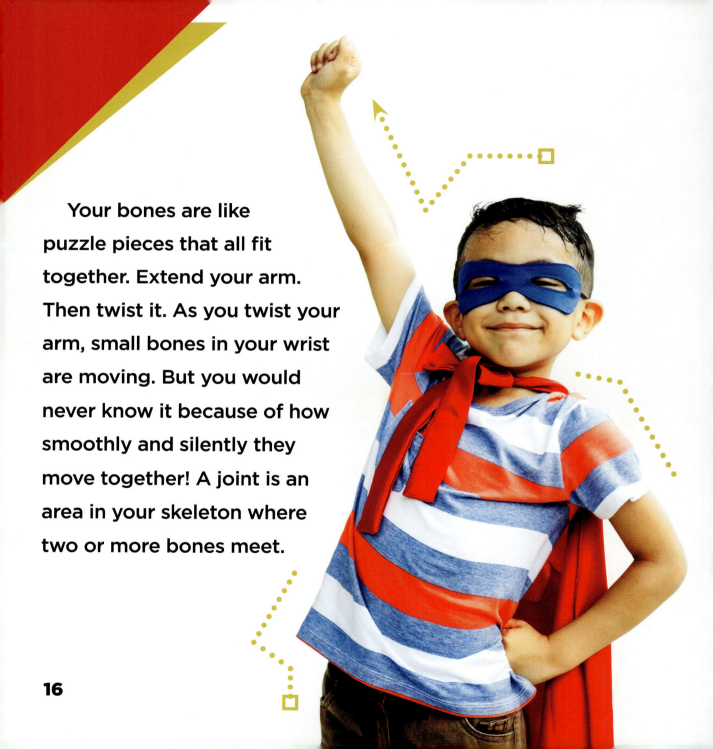

Your bones are like puzzle pieces that all fit together. Extend your arm. Then twist it. As you twist your arm, small bones in your wrist are moving. But you would never know it because of how smoothly and silently they move together! A joint is an area in your skeleton where two or more bones meet.

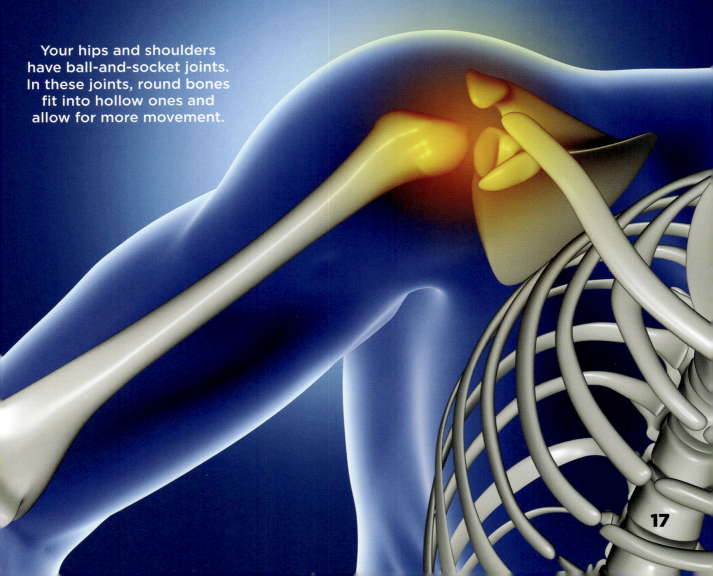

Joints allow you to eat popcorn, ride a bike, and do lots of other things. Some joints move a lot, like your wrists. Other joints, like knees and elbows, move less. They can only move in one direction, like the hinges on a door.

Your hips and shoulders have ball-and-socket joints. In these joints, round bones fit into hollow ones and allow for more movement.

SPINE TIME

Your spine doesn't move a whole lot. It lets you bend over and twist. Its main job is keeping your body upright. Without it, you'd collapse into a blob on the floor. It also protects your spinal cord. This critical bundle of nerves connects your brain to the rest of your body.

Dancers work very hard to have strong, flexible spines.

The spine is not one bone or two—but 33 different bones! The bones are known as vertebrae (VER-tuh-bray). Each one is shaped like a ring and encircles the spinal cord to protect it. In between each vertebra is a disk made from cartilage and other materials. These disks act as cushions. For example, your vertebrae won't slam into one another when you jump.

The spine (shown in white) wraps around the spinal cord (shown in brown).

BRITTLE BONES

Your bones are growing all the time. When you're young, your bones grow fast. As you age, however, your body breaks down old bone faster than it makes new bone. Joints **deteriorate** too. Doctors can replace worn joins with metal or **ceramic** ones. But the new ones aren't as good as a person's own joints.

Older people are also at risk of osteoporosis (os-tee-oh-puh-ROH-sis). Osteoporosis makes your bones weak and more likely to break. However, people with strong bones are less likely to get osteoporosis. And those who eat healthily and exercise have a better chance of keeping their bones healthy. So get moving!

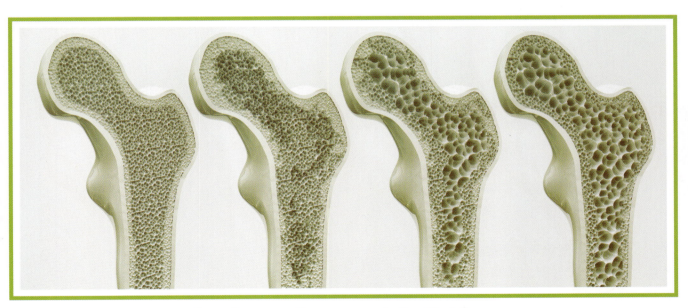

As osteoporosis worsens, holes that form in the cancellous bone get larger.

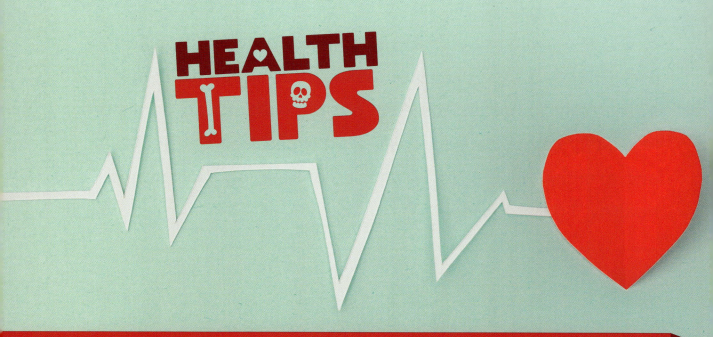

Here are some ways to keep your brain healthy:

- Eat lots of calcium-rich foods, such as leafy green vegetables and nuts.

- Be active! Exercise at least three times a week. Walk, play, bike, jump, or dance.

- Wear a helmet and other safety equipment as needed to protect your bones from injury.

GLOSSARY

ceramic (suh-RAM-ic) relating to products made from clay

collagen (KAH-luh-juhn) the main protein in skin, cartilage, and other connective tissues

deformities (dih-FAWR-mi-teez) when body parts are deformed or misshapen

deteriorate (dih-TEER-ee-uh-reyt) to wear away or to become worse

fused (FYOOZD) joined

mineral (MIN-ur-uhl) a chemical substance, such as iron or zinc, that occurs naturally in certain foods and is important for good health

nerves (NUHRVS) bundles of fibers that pass signals between the brain, spinal cord, or other parts of the body

organs (OR-guhnz) body parts that do a particular job

pneumonia (noo-MOH-nyuh) a disease of the lungs that makes it difficult to breathe

tendons (TEN-duhnz) strong cords that join muscles to bones

tissue (TISH-oo) a group of similar cells that form a part of or an organ in the body

FIND OUT MORE

BOOKS
Balkan, Gabrielle. *Book of Bones*. New York, NY: Phaidon Press, 2017.

Jenkins, Steve. *Bones*. New York, NY: Scholastic, 2010.

Winston, Robert. *The Skeleton Book*. New York, NY: DK, 2016.

WEBSITES
Britannica Kids: Skeletal System
https://kids.britannica.com/kids/article/skeletal-system/353778

National Institutes of Health: Healthy Bones Matter
https://www.niams.nih.gov/health-topics/kids/healthy-bones

National Museum of Natural History: Bone Hall
https://naturalhistory.si.edu/exhibits/bone-hall

INDEX

calcium, 10–11, 15, 22
cancellous, bone, 12–13
cartilage, 15, 19
collagen, 10
deformities, bone, 11
disease, 4–5, 11, 21
Eastlack, Harry, 4–9
FOP, 5–6
joints, 16–17, 20
nerves, 10–11, 19
organs, 9

osteoporosis, 21
periosteum, bone, 12–13
pneumonia, 7
skeleton, 4–9, 16
skull, 6, 8
spine, 6, 18–19
tendons, 6
tissue, 6
vertebrae, 19
vitamin D, 11

ABOUT THE AUTHOR

Joyce Markovics has written hundreds of books for kids. She marvels at the human body—and all the things we still don't know about it. She encourages the young readers of this book to get moving! Your body will thank you. Joyce dedicates this book to her grandmother, Mama, on her 100th birthday.